D0521069

TIME-OUT

...FOR PARENTS

A Compassionate Approach to Parenting

This book is for all the children
who are,
who were,
who will be.

ACKNOWLEDGMENTS

I would like to thank Monique and Brian for their patience and understanding as I continue to learn compassionate parenting.

Melinda and I would like to thank the following people for their ideas, experiences and willingness: Jan Rogerson, Darlene Baumgartner, Jan Leimert, Jan Letendre, Christine Taylor.

And, once again, June Shiver has employed her creative talents to produce a book that we feel most people will find friendly, approachable and downright fun to read. Thank you, June, for your willingness and generosity.

I

INTRODUCTION

As a Zen meditation teacher I teach people to sit in silence facing a blank wall. The idea is to learn to slow down, to become quiet in mind and subtle in attention. This practice can enable us to experience who we really are — our True Nature, our essence, god. Variations of this practice are found in all major religions throughout history.

In the system of controlling children's behavior called "time-out," misbehaving children are isolated, made to be quiet, and sometimes even required to sit facing a wall. This method has been in vogue long enough that I am now receiving students who, when asked to sit quietly by themselves in meditation, feel punished, feel "bad."

My experience is that much of the discussion and literature on parenting focuses on the parent-child interaction, specifically on how to get the child to behave. It seems to me that a vital aspect of the interaction is then neglected, i.e., the parent's internal process.

This book is about changing the concept of time-out. Instead of punishing our children by sending them into isolation, let's offer ourselves time-out to discover our own needs, our own true selves. Then we will have everything <u>we</u> need in order to give our children what <u>they</u> need.

...but wait! What's going on with <u>me</u>?

III

You cannot give to your child
until you can give to yourself!

My hope is that this book will demonstrate how that is so
and encourage a more compassionate way of parenting.

In loving kindness,
Cheri

IV

JAN AND ALIX*

    I had come to dread picking up my 5-year-old daughter Alix each day. I was tense and drained from work pressures and the long commute, and what greeted me every evening at the daycare center was a cranky, whiney, tired, hungry child. It often seemed that her one purpose in life was to make me more miserable.

    I tried saying to Alix the kinds of things I'd heard parents say.

       "Stop whining and crying."

* You will meet Jan and Alix several times throughout the book.

V

"We'll be home in 5 minutes, so stop it now!"

"You've giving me a headache."

Nothing I said seemed to improve the situation. The real message I was giving Alix was that her feelings were not okay.

I so dreaded my daughter's whining and crying that I would steel myself and tough it out, or I would threaten her with "time-out." When my words had no effect on her behavior, I would feel out of control and would resort to raising my voice, which made me feel like I had "lost it." I felt defeated and inadequate; I felt like a bad parent. Many days I would end up with a headache, shouting at my daughter, with her shouting and crying in response.

VI

I tried explaining to Alix what behavior was not okay, e.g., whining, shouting at me, being noncompliant. However, because I was so tired and tense and miserable, I usually was shouting and whining, too! So when explaining appropriate behavior didn't work, I sank to having candy waiting in the car — which made me feel guilty and usually ruined my daughter's appetite for dinner.

I desperately wanted to end our suffering but could not see how to do that. I kept looking for solutions outside myself. I had no reserves left to be calm,

loving and compassionate.

* * *

What We Want for Our Children

The approach to parenting that we are offering is based on this assumption:

That we wish our children to become
   happy, fulfilled individuals
   who grow through life's challenges
   and who feel good about themselves and their lives.

And yet, in working with meditation students, I have become increasingly aware that we are unintentionally teaching our children to be
   self-conscious, emotionally repressed beings
   who believe they are inherently bad.

The reason for this huge difference between what we wish
for our children and how they actually develop is simply that
they are doing what we <u>do</u>, not what we <u>say</u>.

They learn from what we model
and
we model what we learned as children.

Johnny is your
friend. You two
shouldn't fight.

I don't care
what it takes.
I'm going to
get that
account.

I'm so afraid
something awful
is going to
happen.

Don't be silly.
There's nothing
to be afraid of.

If we hope to give children the gift of a happy, responsible, fully alive adulthood, we must first live that way ourselves.

"Yes, but I can't take time for me. The children's needs have to come first."

To this widely held belief I would offer this observation, gleaned from countless airline trips:

 Flight attendant's voice is heard on the pre-flight safety video, as oxygen masks are shown dropping from overhead compartments:

"For those of you who are traveling with small children, be sure to put your oxygen mask on first before assisting your child."

The message is clear: if you aren't alive, you cannot keep your child alive; if a parent's needs are not being met, s/he has no resources to offer the child. But to be alive requires that we pay attention to ourselves in a new way.

☆☆☆☆ At different points along the way through this book we will be signaling you to

STOP

and take "TIME-OUT" to be present to yourself, to your breath, to your feelings, to your experience in the moment.
This is the most powerful
time-out
any of us can take.

Take a moment right now to just BE with yourself. Notice what your breathing is like. Take a few slow, deep breaths, and notice what it's like to be present to all the thoughts and emotions and sensations that you are experiencing. As you breathe, allow your attention to move into your body with your breath: where is there tension? Ask yourself, "What am I feeling?" Notice how you find the answer to that question. Where do you look to find your feelings? Notice your thoughts. What are they saying? Simply be present in this moment, just noticing.

Much of the focus of this little book is on emotion. Our emotions, our feelings are not something to get through, get over, get past, or get away from. Feelings are who we are. We are feeling beings. Feeling is how we know we are alive, how we know we are human.

It is my experience that the process of socialization is an attempt to REMOVE a child's emotions and send the child into adulthood feeling bad and guilty whenever an emotion slips through. The overriding lesson seems to be:

AN ADULT SHOULD BE IN CONTROL.
IT IS NOT POSSIBLE TO BE IN CONTROL
IF YOU ARE EMOTIONAL.

CONCLUSION —
GET RID OF EMOTION
BECAUSE EMOTION THREATENS CONTROL.

EMOTION
THREATENS YOUR ABILITY
TO BE WHO YOU SHOULD BE!

OR, as a child learns it: IT IS BAD TO FEEL.

Think about some common messages from your childhood, and consider the times you might have passed them along to your children.

- Big girls/boys don't cry.
- Stop crying. There's nothing to cry about.
- Don't be afraid. There's nothing to be afraid of.
- Don't be shy.
- Stop feeling sorry for yourself.
- You can't be hungry - you just ate.
- You're just trying to get attention.

With such messages, we deny a child's experience of him- or herself. We are saying, "Don't have your feelings, have the feelings I want you to have," or "Don't be who you are, be who I want you to be."

But please,

no guilt here.

Guilt is part of the whole system of control, and it misses the point altogether.

Instead of feeling guilty, consider how the messages from your childhood offer a way of seeing what happened to you – and notice that how you are treating your child is usually how _you_ were treated.

Consider that how you are treating your child is probably how you were treated.

Take a moment to remember some messages from your childhood. Jot them down, and notice how you feel as you recall how your feelings were negated.

_____

_____

_____

_____

_____

_____

Human beings are feeling beings, and to be fully human is
to have the experience of the full range of emotions,
from happiness to sadness
from grief and rage
to joy and awe.

Emotions, when we take the time to explore
and experience them, are in our
internal landscapes
like weather is in the world
around us:
ranging from dark and cloudy and stormy
to bright and calm and sunny,
constantly changing, rarely the same for very long.

14

Most of us, however, were raised to believe that there are "good" feelings and "bad" feelings (just as forecasters predict "good" weather and "bad" weather), and that the successful adult is always happy,
always has good feelings,
while the person who fails at adulthood
has bad feelings —
and, worst of all, can't control them.

I have come to understand this conditioning as the origin of self-hate, because to be taught that my feelings are bad is the same as being taught that I am bad.

We are trained from early childhood to hide unacceptable feelings, which results in depressing all our feelings. It is possible to keep a lid on our feelings —
but not selectively.
Keep one kind of feeling hidden,
and they all remain hidden.

As a result, many of us reach adulthood having learned to depress our feelings and now struggle with the guilt and shame and hopelessness of depression.

It is not possible to depress our feelings
and not be depressed.

16

TIME-OUT

Sometime in the early 1960s the word began to get out that hitting a child as a means of discipline not only was abusive to the child, but also was ineffective as a method of educating the child in "proper" behavior. What hitting taught children most effectively was that it is okay to hit other people.

Behavior specialists then began to promote the idea of "time-out." If your child is misbehaving, being difficult, in need of discipline, send the child to his or her room alone, set a timer, and allow the child back into relationship with you either when the timer goes off, or when the child "improves" the behavior (that is, has stopped doing whatever it was that was driving you crazy!)

"I can't take anymore!"X

When a parent sends a child into time-out, the scenario is often one where the parent feels stretched to the absolute limit by some behavior of the child — feels, in fact, as though she or he (the parent) is about to "lose it," because it seems the child is "out of control."

But what does it mean to "lose it?"
Lose what?

18

The parent is upset because she or he feels unable to control the child. The parent needs a break from the child and has the power to send the child away. When the child is gone, the adult **FEELS** more in control. It **SEEMS** to be working.

WHEW!

19

Take a moment now to recall how you felt the last time you thought you were about to "lose it." What was going on inside you? How did your body feel? What were you saying to yourself?

It's okay to "lose it."
It's one way to get in touch with your feelings.

No need for guilt.
Parenting can be difficult.

Be gentle with yourself
as you would be with your own child
or another loved one.

The idea of losing control assumes that we are in control, and I believe this is where the breakdown occurs. Parents "lose it" because they believe they are supposed to be "in control." We are taught to believe that adults are in control, or should be.

But control is an illusion; there is no such thing as control, only the appearance of control which is maintained by pushing our feelings down, by "flatlining" our emotions.

I would like to suggest that the real loss happens long before we feel we are about to "lose it."

THE REAL LOSS
is not having the full experience of
OURSELVES,
of our FEELING selves.

When the adult begins to feel she or he is about to lose it, what is really happening is that the feelings that are always there and depressed are threatening to break through and be seen, to be consciously felt.

We are conditioned, however, to Be Happy. If we are happy, we believe that we are good or are doing it right. If we are sad or mad or confused or afraid, we have been taught to feel that we are bad, or are doing it wrong.

So we learn to be even-tempered, never to be "out of control," which is seen as being "childish."

The belief is that to have your emotions take over makes you a bad person, so we become masters at rationalizing ourselves out of our feelings.

Therefore,

a "good" parent teaches the child:

ALWAYS KEEP IT TOGETHER.

And when,
inevitably,
the parent loses it,
and explodes,
she hates herself and feels guilty,
feels like a bad parent.

JAN AND ALIX CONTINUED

    It never occurred to me to look inward, to myself, to see what needs of mine were not being met. I did not realize how tired and drained I was — that I actually had nothing left for Alix. I took her behavior as a personal attack, and the interaction between us degenerated into a power struggle.

* * *

Go inside yourself for a moment, and notice what your breath is like. Are you breathing? Notice the quality of your breath: is it slow, fast, even, irregular? What are you feeling, right at this moment? How do you know what you are feeling? What gives you the answer to that question?

That feeling of about-to-lose-it is actually a gift: it is the self signaling itself that a need is being neglected.

It is sort of like emotional hunger pangs. When you get really hungry, you do not consider that you have "lost it." You might have learned that it is helpful not to get that hungry, because when you do you tend to gobble your food, eat the wrong things, overeat — it's not a good system.

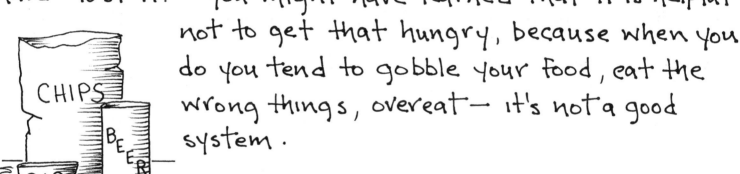

But does letting yourself get that hungry make you a bad person?

No, of course not. It makes you a person who is out of touch with your body.

When you get to the point of screaming with anger or frustration, does this make you a bad person? No. It makes you a person who is out of touch with your feelings.

Screaming, then, is to emotions
as gobbling is to hunger.

When we've gone too long without a basic need being met, our reactions become **HUGE.**

So, there you are screaming, and you say,

"Well, I'm certainly in touch with my feelings Now!"

Stop and ask yourself:

"What happened right before that?"
"When could I have noticed?"
"What signals was I getting that I was upset?"

With practice you will be able to notice these signals earlier and earlier.

CYNTHIA AND RICKY

Cynthia told about the afternoon she slid the refrigerator into its new home in the kitchen — only to discover that in the process she had torn up a section of newly laid linoleum. She was upset, but just continued arranging things in the kitchen — until her four-year-old son Ricky began pounding the pegs into his toddler's carpentry set. And pounding. And pounding.

She found herself screaming at him, "Stop that awful noise! You're giving me a headache!" She stopped to take a breath after she heard herself, and realized almost immediately that the screaming at Ricky was really screaming

31

about the torn linoleum. Ricky was just playing carpenter, and most days she would have encouraged him with comments like, "Aren't you having fun!" But today she had depressed the feelings of sadness and anger and disappointment about the torn linoleum, and those feelings found the next available outlet in "losing it" over Ricky's pounding.

"Losing control" is really about <u>finding</u> feelings that have been neglected and now refuse to be ignored.

The crucial information
is what happens
inside ourselves
<u>right</u> <u>before</u> we "lose it."

Take a few deep breaths, allowing your attention to rest gently on your breathing. If you notice places of tension in your body, simply let your breath embrace those places, so that when you breathe out you feel the tension dissolving. Quietly ask, "What feeling have I been ignoring or avoiding?"

Of course, it's natural to avoid our feelings if we find them uncomfortable. It takes practice to get in touch with them and more practice to accept them for what they are. One step at a time, that's all that is needed.

And, you are doing it.

How Can We Teach Our Children What We Want Them to Learn?

The **HOW** of teaching children what we really hope they will learn

is astonishingly simple:

We must learn to BE – to live – the way we want them to be. We must begin to find out who <u>we</u> really are beneath the social conditioning we have lived with all of our lives.

How do you want your child to be as an adult? Do you want your child to be repressed, to feel anxious and fearful of losing control? If that is the adult you want to produce, then be that way with your child.

If you want a child who has the full range of his or her emotions, then you must begin to allow yourself the full range of _your_ emotions.

Once you are able to do that, and to know that emotions are to be welcomed, not rejected, then your child will learn to do the same.

You must take care of the
child inside your adult self
BEFORE you will be able to
take care of the child or
children you are raising.

These steps can help us teach our children what we want them to learn:

Being with _ourselves_

Being ourselves _with_ our children

Allowing our children to be _themselves_

Being With Yourself: Receiving

Consider the infant with its very basic needs. When we hear it cry, we listen for a moment to try to hear the need being expressed.
Is the baby hungry?
        tired?

        wet?

        in pain?

        in need of company?
We attune as keenly as we can to determine what the need is, and then we respond with food,
                a fresh diaper,

                some cuddle time,
with whatever seems most likely to bring comfort to the child.

41

What if we were as keenly attuned to,
and as motivated to respond to,
OUR OWN NEEDS?

What if I notice a feeling (hear the cry), attune as keenly as I can to what is being expressed (Am I angry, overwhelmed, hurt, sad, frightened...?) and then respond to the need as appropriate?

Often all that is needed is for the feeling to be acknowledged and accepted, to be given my undivided attention — to simply be allowed to exist. So I might say to myself, "Oh, you're sad. Well, what would help right now?"
or
"What's making you sad?"

42

Ask yourself:

What am I experiencing in this moment?

What am I seeing? What am I hearing?

What sensations are happening in my body?

Where are they happening? What emotions am I experiencing?

Can I accept how I am feeling? What do I need right now?

    Notice whatever comes up and try seeing each moment of attention as a junction with two possible paths:

   one leading to the same old suffering

   another leading away from the same old suffering —

                        toward acceptance

                        and freedom.

I would like to suggest that our unrecognized, unacknowledged feelings are crying out just as an infant might, and expressing the same need:
to be acknowledged and responded to,
to be heard and accepted.

"Yes but,
how can I learn to notice, respond to, and accept my feelings? This sounds so foreign to my way of being in the world."

Most of us act out of the conditioning we received as children much of which turned us away from ourselves and focused our attention outward.

That's okay, it's just helpful information to have because, in becoming conscious, we learn to turn our attention back inward and to find compassion for ourselves and our feelings.

Here are some steps we have found helpful.

1. Find the willingness to be present to your inner self. Just as you have the ability to distinguish your child's cry from all the other noises and sounds in the world, you can be available to your inner child, you can develop the same receptive awareness for your own needs and feelings. Stay present and attentive long enough to recognize whatever is there.

2. Notice/acknowledge that there is a need or feeling, something inside that wants attention. — It not only is okay to want attention (something that's hard to accept after years of hearing, "You're just trying to get attention!"), it seems that getting attention is an often-neglected though essential human need.

3. Attune to what is needed. Just as you developed the capacity to tell the difference between your baby's cries of pain, hunger and discomfort, allow yourself to hear/feel the differences between your internal, feeling experiences.

4. Respond with what seems most needed. This is often as simple (and as hard) as accepting what you feel, without judging it, without trying to change it, without hating yourself for it.

We have all had the experience of being with a child who falls down and skins his knee when Mom is out of hearing range. The child will cry for a moment or two and then seem okay again — until Mom comes into sight.

Then the tears start up, more agonized than ever. Mom comforts the child, and all is well once more. The little boy seems only to need Mom to notice, attend to, feel sorry with (attune to) and respond gently and nonjudgmentally to the skinned knee, then life can go on.

Practice the four steps whenever there is a moment:

- When you first wake up
- In the shower
- As you take a walk
- As you drive to work
- In line at the bank
- During a TV commercial
- _____
- _____
- _____

Plan a few minutes each day as your exclusive time-out. Try to treat this time as a gift to yourself, rather than as another should to burden your life. It's important to have quiet, alone time to create the inner peace that our selves long to experience. Daily life, particularly for parents, is so filled with distractions and "must-do" activities that the opportunity for this kind of time-out gets lost in the shuffle.

And,

it may be the most important thing
you have ever done for yourself!

Because beginning to notice, acknowledge and accept our inner feeling worlds requires practicing away from the normal insanity of everyday life. By practicing these four steps

In a quiet place, it will become more possible to follow them when the kids are bouncing off the walls, dinner is late, and you're exhausted from a busy day at work.

Whenever your awareness settles on your inner process, allow that awareness to expand to include how you're feeling, into fully noticing your experience in the moment. You don't need to try to <u>change</u> your experience. It's just helpful to <u>become aware</u> of what's going on.

Once the idea of giving yourself time-out has settled just a little bit into your consciousness, it will be easier at times of stress for that critical pause to happen, the pause that creates the space for you to fully experience yourself. Then, the next time you find yourself yelling at your kids and going into the countdown to explosion —

"I told you…"

"I need for you to…"

"You need to listen to me…"

"I'm warning you…"

"If you don't _____ right now…"

"How many times do I have to tell you…"

"One…two…"

— you'll increase your chances of stopping and modeling for your children the ways you hope they will treat themselves and those they love.

For a moment turn your attention inward. What are you saying to yourself? How are you feeling?  What is your breath like? Your heart rate? Is there tension in your body? Do you want to scream? Cry? Throw things? What are your thoughts like? Are you scrambling for control? Are you trying to talk yourself out of what you are feeling? Can you accept whatever you are feeling and thinking? If not, how do you know it's not okay to feel what you are feeling and think what you are thinking?

JAN AND ALIX CONTINUED

As I began to look inside and ask myself what I was feeling, I saw these emotions:

- anger at my burdens (job, single parenthood, my daughter's "bad" behavior)
- sadness and hurt that she would treat me this way
- hate for the whole situation and resistance toward it
- despair because this was not an acceptable way to be with my daughter

On top of that, physically I was feeling tired and hungry.

✳ ✳ ✳

"Once I've seen what my feelings and needs are, how can I respond? What I really need is a vacation, and there is no time or money for it!"

Check back with this voice that says, "I need a vacation." What would a vacation do for you? Usually, if we listen very, very closely to what we are asking of our kids at times when we're exasperated, what we are wanting from them is exactly what we need to provide for ourselves.

What "I need a vacation" really expresses may be most

perfectly captured in those familiar words

"You need to listen to me!"

– directed not to our children but to the parts of ourselves that are too busy to stop and listen to the voice within.

The following is an exercise we have found helpful in guiding us to the responses that our deepest selves

long to receive.

Imagine that you are with an infant or very small child, or with a puppy or kitten. As images arise, choose the one that tugs hardest at your heart, the one that you feel most deeply.

Now imagine that the little creature you're with is very upset, sad, hurt, or lonely. What would you say to that little being? How would you comfort it?

Can you find ways to be with this helpless little one that allow it to feel fully accepted by you?

Take a little time to find ways of responding that feel right for you. Now, try saying these same things to yourself, to your own needful inner self.

→ WHAT IS THAT EXPERIENCE LIKE FOR YOU?

Take a few moments to write down your responses.

Here are some of the phrases that others have come up with to say when doing the exercise on page 59:

"I love you."

"It's okay to feel what you're feeling."

"I know you're afraid. I won't leave you."

"I won't abandon you no matter what."

"You are doing the best you can."

"I understand."

A vacation <u>would</u> be nice, and since it isn't possible, perhaps your inner self would like to hear,

  "I know you'd like a vacation, and it's really frustrating not to be able to get it."

It would like to hear that <u>you</u>
understand and accept how it's feeling.

Is it time to give yourself a break?

Are you ready for some

TIME-OUT?

Here are some suggestions for time-out activities:

-Imagine that you are a balloon. Focus on your breathing, feeling the air as it enters your body and fills it completely. Feel the air as it leaves your body. Take ten breaths like this, just noticing what it's like to feel like a balloon.

-Label what you are feeling without using thought words. For instance, instead of "I feel angry," you might say, "I'm going to explode. I feel like a volcano." Or, "I want to scream." Or, "I feel like a dinosaur is sitting on my chest." Let your feelings express themselves in images instead of abstracts. Focus your attention on your feelings instead of depressing them. Find a safe way to let the energy out.

- Scream into a pillow, or sit in the car with the windows rolled up and scream.

- Pound a mattress with your fists.

- Dance, using every part of your body as energetically as possible (and pick music you really like!)

- Run around the block as fast as you can.

- Again!

- Write about what you are feeling.

- Get out the crayons and draw pictures of your feelings.

CRAYONS

-How about some ideas that come from inside yourself?

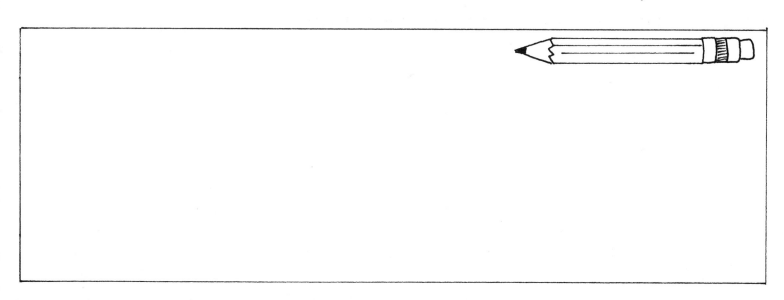

It's okay to take time for yourself, to take care of yourself. In fact, it's the best thing you can do for yourself... and everyone you love.

Being With Your Child: Modeling Self-Acceptance

When a parent is
   being true to himself or herself,
   being at-one-with,
the child knows it and can sense the parent
being attuned inwardly.

This is the place we call CENTER.

Recall times when you are feeling calm and centered and, from that place, tell your child <u>no</u> in response to some request or behavior. Now remember times when you are not so centered, perhaps are grumpy and feeling overburdened, and tell your child no from that place.

How are those experiences different for you? Can you remember how you feel each time? How does your child respond to you in each situation?

Yes, it feels wonderful to be centered and to act from that place. But when we are stressed and off center in our feelings and actions,

the best we can do
is to accept that that's where we are.

It's not easy being a parent. We must be our own best friends, accepting ourselves however we are.
And it's from that place
of acceptance and compassion
that we can best model for our children.

71

Many adults believe it is upsetting to a child to experience an adult having an emotion like anger or sadness or fear. Yet how will a child ever learn to be okay with her or his feelings if all that is modeled is adults trying to pretend they aren't having feelings?

When we can be ourselves with our children, they will learn how to be themselves, because they will learn the self-acceptance we are modeling for them.

RACHEL AND JASON

When Rachel discovered that everything she had carefully packed in the car for a trip had been rearranged and nothing could be found, she let out a spontaneous yell and stomped her feet in frustration. She quickly looked at her four-year-old son, concerned that her outburst might have frightened him, even though it wasn't directed at him. To her surprise, she saw that he was simply watching her with interest, and that he then went on with his own activities. It seemed that he knew Mom was just angry: nothing to fear, nothing to hide. Mom was just expressing her feelings.

As we become aware of our internal experience during difficult interactions with our children, we see that the same situations arise again and again.

And although the repetition is exasperating, it is a golden opportunity to really get it that the way we are responding

not only doesn't work

but never has,

and this awareness frees us to try something new.

Whenever your attention is caught and the awareness comes, "It's happening again," that is a point at which to begin. Just as you've begun to ask yourself,

"What do I need?"

you can ask out loud, including your child in the question,

"What would help us right now?"

—Let's take time-out together.

—Let's scream into a pillow together. Or sit in the car with the windows up and scream.

—Let's pound a mattress with our fists.

—Let's dance, using every part of our bodies as energetically as possible and pick music we really like.

—Let's run around the block as fast as we can.

—Again!

—Let's get out the crayons and draw pictures of our feelings.

—Let's take turns lying with our heads on each other's stomachs making silly sounds until we get the giggles.

Let's come up with some ideas that are just for us.

When we watch closely enough to begin to interrupt the patterns with new responses, it often happens that other repetitive interactions begin to shift, too.

New responses arise and the energy between parent and child changes
from the energy of conflict
to the energy of mutual enjoyment.

Allowing Our Children to Be Themselves

Once you have found ways to be with your feelings in an accepting way,

and once you have found ways of truly being yourself with your child,

the next step
is learning how to be with your child's feelings.

And the answer is quite simple: be with him or her in the same way you have learned to be with your own inner child —
pay attention
be attuned
respond in a caring way.

Johnny is begging for that ice cream cone and it's almost dinner time so you tell him, "No, this isn't a good time for ice cream." Can you just let him have his feelings – disappointment, anger, sadness? "I know you're sad (or mad, or both), Johnny. It's okay to be mad, and sometimes we can't have what we want."

Notice.
Accept.
Respond caringly.

80

JAN AND ALIX CONTINUED

Once I could look at my own feelings, it was easy to see that Alix was behaving the way she was because she was feeling emotions not too different from mine:

- anger that she had been needing to be good all day
- sadness because she missed me and needed my attention
- safe in my presence to express herself after enduring the restraints of school all day

As for physical feelings, she too was tired and hungry.

***

Allowing a child to be her or himself does not mean the child is given license to behave in whatever ways she or he wishes. It is important for both the child and the parent to know that the parent is always boss; that there are acceptable and unacceptable behaviors; that there are family rules that everyone, parents and children, must abide by.

Having feelings and <u>acting</u> on them
are two very different things,
and it is crucial to understand the difference.

We often confuse feelings with actions:

· I can't have angry feelings or I'll hurt someone.

· I can't allow my sexual feelings to be conscious, or I'll become promiscuous.

· I can't let myself feel my sadness, or I'll start crying and never be able to stop.

· I can't be too happy or I'll bother the people around me.

In fact, to feel my feelings I do not have to do anything or involve anyone else at all. We live in fear of our feelings, however, believing that if we allow ourselves to experience them, we'll run amok. The belief is:

if feelings are controlled,
behavior is controlled.

Yet it is my experience that just the opposite is true:
when feelings are controlled,
behavior runs amok.

When I depress my anger, sooner or later I find myself screaming at someone..

When I'm not afraid of my feelings,
when they are allowed to exist,
        it seems that they limit themselves.

When I just let the energy of anger be there,
noticing how it registers
in my thoughts
and in my body,

It seems to go on for a while
            and then be finished.

If I learn to use that energy in a way that benefits me, I will soon see that the emotion isn't destructive at all. In fact, it's quite instructive.

One of my favorite things to do when life is getting to me is to turn on loud, fast music and clean house, top to bottom. Before long, I'm no longer upset, the energy is dissipated, I've had a good time with myself, and I have a clean house.

What is your experience of a feeling?
What happens when you allow a feeling to arise,
be noticed, be felt, and not be acted upon?
See if you are able to find the willingness to let a feeling
just be a kind of energy and not something you have to act
on in any particular way.

As with any thing new, <u>this</u> <u>work</u> <u>takes</u> <u>practice</u>. We must learn to attune to our own needs, to hear and be with the child within us.

We no longer need to see ourselves as "losing it." Instead, we are learning to find and reclaim the parts of us that were taken away so many years ago when we were taught that what we feel is bad.

We are learning to accept ourselves.

If we want to reassure ourselves that there is
   nothing bad,
   nothing wrong with us,
   all the way down to the depths
                              of our being,

all we need to do is recall the sweetness, defenselessness and
innocence of the children we love. This proves to us that
         the essence of a being
            is goodness.

The only way we will ever stop
the abuse and neglect of children
is to stop believing
that punishing people
makes them good.

Punishing children does not make them good, just as punishing
ourselves does not make us good. It is the belief that we need
to be punished that prevents us from seeing that

We are already GOOD.

JAN AND ALIX

Paying attention to and accepting my own feelings and my daughter's dissolved the tightness and resistance and allowed me to open to other possibilities.

- I fully acknowledged my feelings to myself and fully accepted them as being okay.
- I fully acknowledged my daughter's feelings by asking her how she was feeling and letting her know it was okay to feel the way she did.

We treated our trip home differently—

prepacking a nutritious snack and going to a park near Alix's school before starting the drive. A wonderful new routine! I was able to drop my previous belief that this was impossible because I don't have time; I have to get home and cook; do laundry; make calls; help Alix, etc.

Because we had both let go of so much suffering, we were energized by the new experience and arrived home happy and relaxed.

How I am with myself has made the difference. For me, the world has become a much friendlier place.

Workshops and retreats based on compassionate parenting and many other subjects are offered by Cheri Huber, Melinda Guyol, and others at the Zen Monastery Practice Center near Murphys, California, in the foothills of the Sierra Nevadas. "Kids Retreats," including parents, are held during summer months.

For a current schedule, write P.O. Box 1979, Murphys, CA, 95247, fax 209-728-0861, email zencentr@volcano.net, or visit www.keepitsimple.org on the internet.

For a one-year subscription to the Center's quarterly newsletter, In Our Practice, send a check for $12.00 along with your name and address.